Knowing Hekate
A spiritual coloring experience

Sara Croft

This project would never have been accomplished without the guidance and support of many individuals. I dedicate this book to my husband, who serves as a guiding light in my life. To C. Tidball, Mega Meg, Hazel Holbrook, Tina, Maggie, and Linda, all my gratitude for looking over what I had and for the suggestions.

Hekate is the goddess of three-way crossroads, and lady who presides over thresholds of all sorts. Her origins are in either Thrace (modern Bulgaria, more or less) or Caria (modern south-western Turkey). Her most common surviving image shows her as three young women back to back, holding keys, torches, jars, or other tools. Hesiod, the 8th c. BCE Greek poet, tells us that she has dominion in the sea, sky, and earth. Her worship eventually stretched across the span of the Mediterranean, and expanded to include a great range of characteristics. She is the Goddess of Witches, who guides the dead into the afterlife, and who works her wisdom in childbirth. She is also, for some, a Savior Goddess, who brings light into the darkness.

With so much variety in her history, it is no surprise that she has a diversity of symbols, including Hekate's Wheel, or Strophalos. The Wheel was discovered as a button design from Mycenae, unrelated to Hekate, but somehow, it has become one of her most popular representations.

Hekate is Dadophoros, the Torchbearer. Many of her epithets are related to light and to fire. For many of her devotees, this light is central to her nature.

She is the light on the dark road through life, and the guide who walks with us through both birth and death.

There are many meditative exercises that can help one connect with the Gods. Creating designs with their symbols being but one. This illustration gives Hekate's name in the original Greek, as well as showing her dominion over Earth (Chthonian), Sea (Einalian), and Heaven (Ouranian). Of beginnings and endings, and spanning all the realms, Hekate can also be seen associated with a variety of animals, including the lion, horse, and dog. Symbols such as these can serve as sources of insight.

Hesiod wrote the Theogony in the 8th century BCE. Hekate's tale serves as a critical pivot in the flow of the story. It is there that we learn that she is sometimes known to be the daughter of the Titans Asteria and Perses. Asteria is a goddess of the stars, and she is associated with prophecy. Hekate's father, Perses, is less well known in the modern world. It seems that he has associations with destruction and war.

Both of these domains are also seen in Hekate, as she is known to provide insight into oracles, and was important in the war against the Titans as a fighter herself.

In the Orphic Argonautika (5th-6th c. CE) we find a lush description of the sanctuary to Hekate in the city of Colchis, where Medea hails. One of the city gates, by which no one entered was where the sanctuary stood, a host to a vast garden full of trees, medicinal herbs, and poisons.

Here we see a small selection of the trees which are associated with her in some way: oak, black poplar, almond, cypress, yew, among many others.

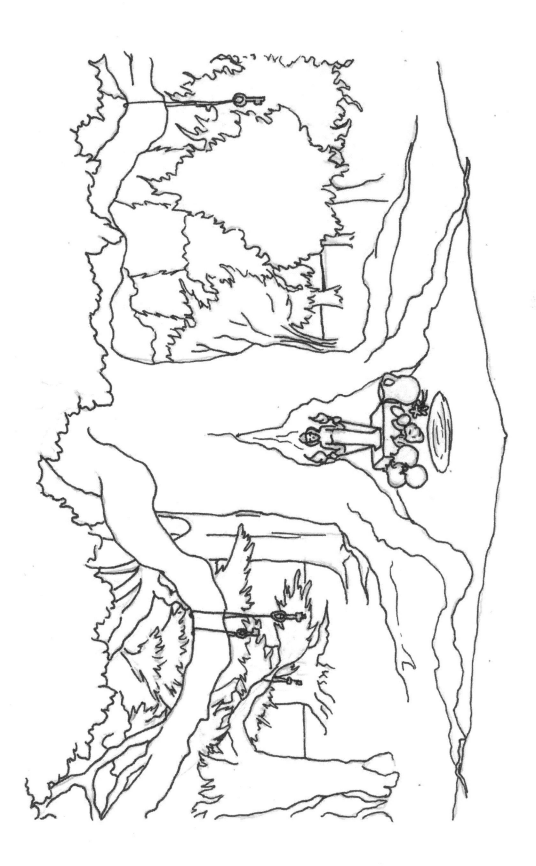

Hekate is definitely a triple goddess, though many see it as a metaphor for her ability to see in all directions. Unlike the modern archetype of Mother, Maiden, Crone, the triplicity of Hekate is of three young ladies. In ancient art, when shown in three, she bears the same face in all three aspects, and often carries the same tools.

Here we see three devotees standing together to serve as symbolic representations of that triplicity.

Many different animals are associated with Hekate historically, but modern practitioners have given her some new friends. As creatures of the night, the bat and owl have come to join Hekate's train, as has the noisy scavenger raven. For the Greeks, the raven has always been Apollo's bird. The owl is best known as Athena's. And the bat is closely associated with the Dream gods as well as playing a part in a story of Dionysos.

Yet, many devotees have adopted these very animals as the associates of the night-wandering Hekate.

Several ancient authors saw Hekate not as the daughter of Asteria and Perses, but as one of the many children of Nox, or Nyx, the Night.

Hekate, according to Hesiod, has power over the unfruitful sea. As a goddess of boundaries and borders, here we see her standing on the shore in the night sky, with storms gathering on the horizon. Will she bring fish to the fisherman? Will she send the storms to crash upon the shore?

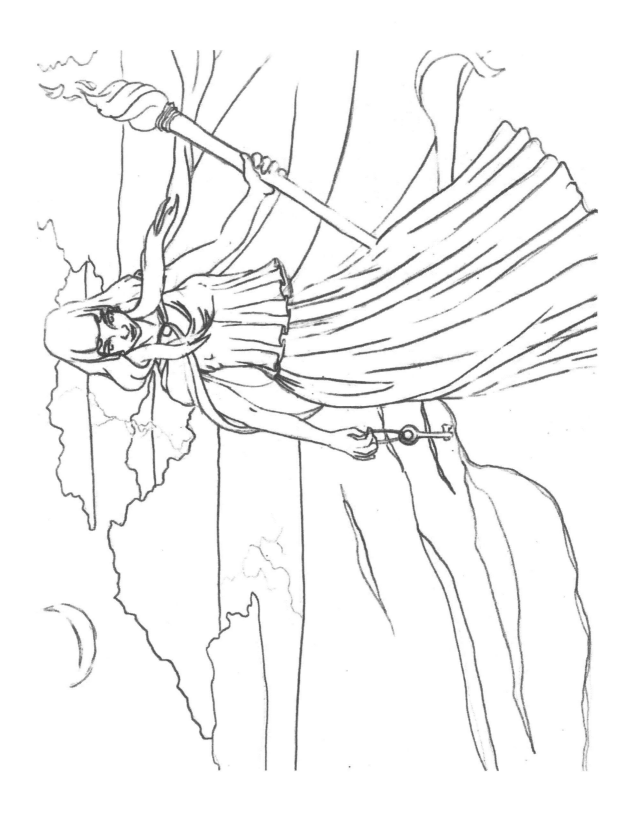

Hekate's grace extends to many plants. Thuja occidentalis, barley, is associated with all of the gods, and was one of the main offerings given in the ancient world. Each participant tossed a handful of barley on the fire at the beginning of each rite. Cardamom (elettaria cardamomum) is today a little-used kitchen spice, but is one of the plants listed in the Orphic Argonautika, along with Lesser Celandine (ranunculus ficaria). Lastly, almond (prunus dulcis) is likewise a suitable offering. Prior to cultivation, this tree produced a poisonous seed. Only by our hand has it become the healthy treat it is today.

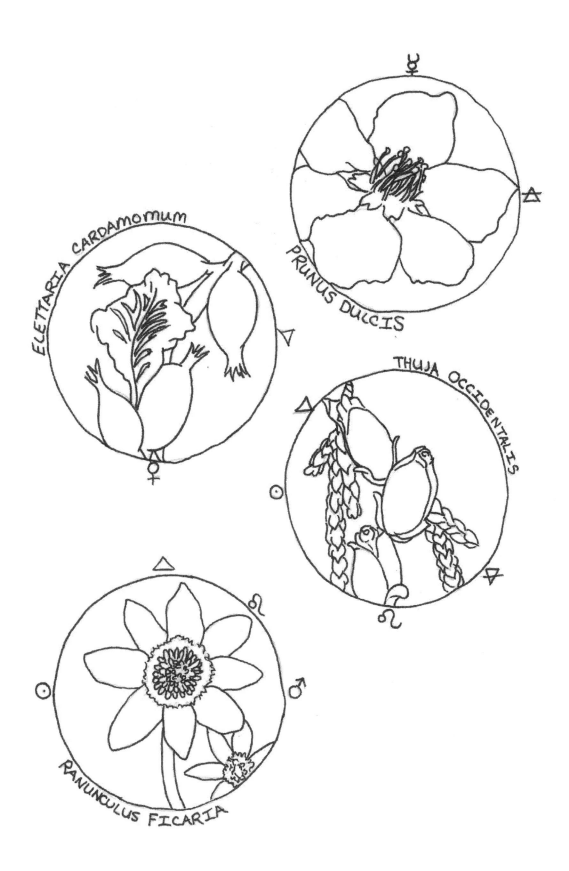

ELETTARIA CARDAMOMUM

PRUNUS DULCIS

THUJA OCCIDENTALIS

RANUNCULUS FICARIA

Hekate guides the souls of the dead out of this world and into the afterlife, just as she leads the newborn spirits into this world. She is both a psychopomp (literally, soul walker) and an eileithyia (one of the goddesses associated with childbirth), because she holds the key to all doors.

Late in antiquity, we find Hekate's image often has animal heads. Along with this diversification of imagery, we also see her domains have expanded. She is said to command winds, fire, earth, and waters, to hold the keys to life and death, to be a Goddess of the home, and of the afterlife. She becomes, for many, Soul itself.

Among her animals, we find the goat, the lion, and most often, the
snake.

When Persephone was taken by Hades for wife without Demeter's knowledge, the grain goddess was stricken with despair, so says the Homeric Hymn to Demeter (7th c. BCE). It was Hekate who heard what happened, who listened to the cries of the Kore. The gentle maiden approached Demeter (who is sometimes called Hekate's mother) and suggested that they seek out the Sun, Helios, because he sees all things. Together they went to Helios, and, thanks to Hekate, eventually mother and daughter were reunited. Though Persephone has to return to Hades' care from time to time, Hekate always travels with her.

In some rarer circumstances, we see Hekate described as amphiprosopos, two-headed, like the Roman god Janus.

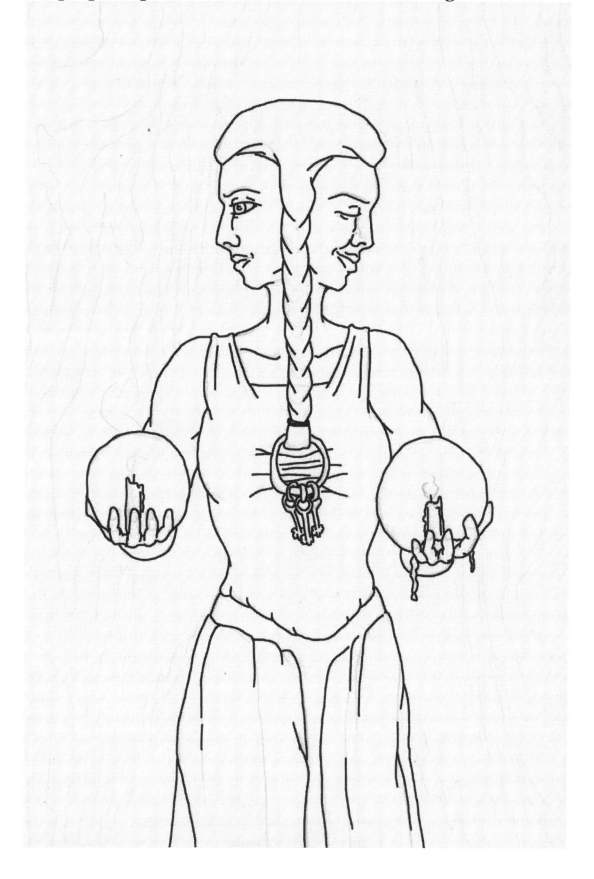

From the earliest days, Hekate is described as working with Hermes in the fields. They share many occupations and attributes, both guiding the dead into the underworld, and serving as messengers. They are both gods of the roadways and crossroads. Some of the ancients believed they were lovers, and that their son was the Hero Eleusis. The Roman author Propertius even goes so far as to describe her as being deflowered by Hermes.

There exists speculation that Hekate is one of the goddesses that can be called the Mistress of Animals, or Potnia Theron. It is possible that this role is born out of some overlap with Artemis, which was extensive and caused the two to have many merging characteristics.

The Orphic Argonautika also tells us that Hekate's sanctuary had mugwort (artemisia vulgaris), the poppy (papaver somniferum), and valerian (valeriana officinalis). In many of the surviving descriptions of the afterlife, we hear tell of the blooming asphodel (asphodelus ramosus), and so this too is one of her plants.

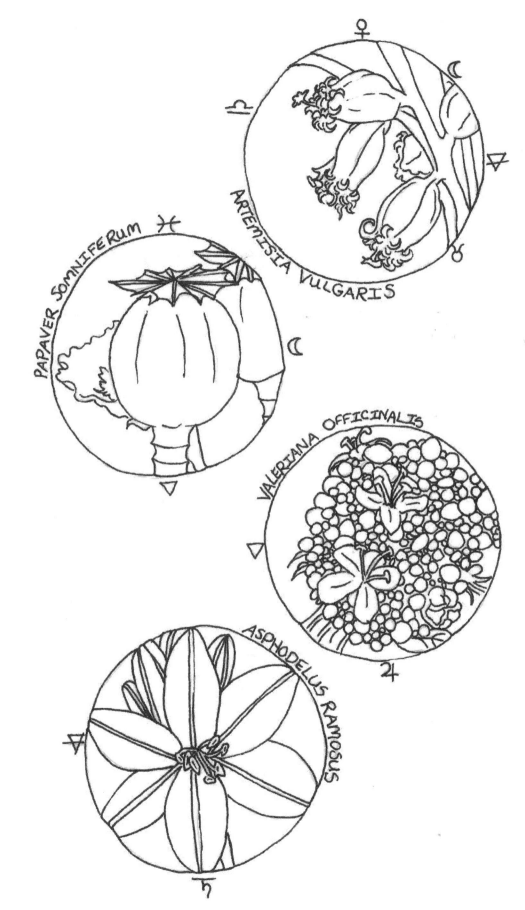

ARTEMISIA VULGARIS

PAPAVER SOMNIFERUM

VALERIANA OFFICINALIS

ASPHODELUS RAMOSUS

Hekate and Poseidon work together to bring the fisherman his crop.

Sometimes in meditation one is inspired. This is based loosely on one such moment I had with Hekate. It took me a while to parse. Hekate brings light to our lives, showing us the truth, but it is we who must choose and act. We must take the sword of our Wills and use the tools at our disposal.

Hekate bears many descriptions that highlight her triplicity. She is three-necked, three-faced, three-headed, three-formed, and three-bodied. Many of the surviving images of Her show us a maiden back to back to back, or around a column.

Of the many different species associated with Hekate, few are mentioned as often as the hound, horse, and cattle. Hekate is cow-eyed, an epithet emphasizing her beauty. Her association with the horse may reflect her relationship with the sea, as Poseidon is the creator of the equine. In late antiquity, we find descriptions of Her with the heads of these creatures.

In Hekate's most celebrated temple, in Lagina, Caria (modern day Mugla, Turkey), Hekate was closely aligned with the nearby cult of Zeus Panamaros, which was based the next town over. Together, they were attributed with saving the region from invasion and disease.

Ζευς
Παναμαρος

Έκατη
Λαγινιτις

Στρατονικεία
Λαγινα
Παναμαρα

Hekate is the Keybearer. In Athens she had shrines in front of many houses, where she served a protective function. Even at temples, she sometimes had a presence at the entrances. As a keybearer, Hekate protects and allows entrance where she wills. She is the possessor of the key to the House of Hades, and some even say that she can unlock the entirety of the cosmos.

In the Hymn to Demeter, it is Hekate to leads the Grain Goddess to seek Helios, the Titan of the Sun, who sees all. He is described in Sophocles' *The Root Cutters* as "the Spear of Hekate of the Crossroads".

Hekate's domains expanded over the millennia of her worship. By late antiquity, she is called Pasikrateia, "Universal Queen." Yet, we see something of this in Hesiod as well, as she has dominion over her portion of each of the three realms. She is Chthonic, yes, but she is also Heavenly. Here she holds the Moon in her hands, spanning the sky above us.

Hekate's garden grows thick with dangerous plants that may heal or harm. We find Mandrake, Wolfsbane, Belladonna, and Foxglove all blossoming there. Each are deadly, and beautiful.

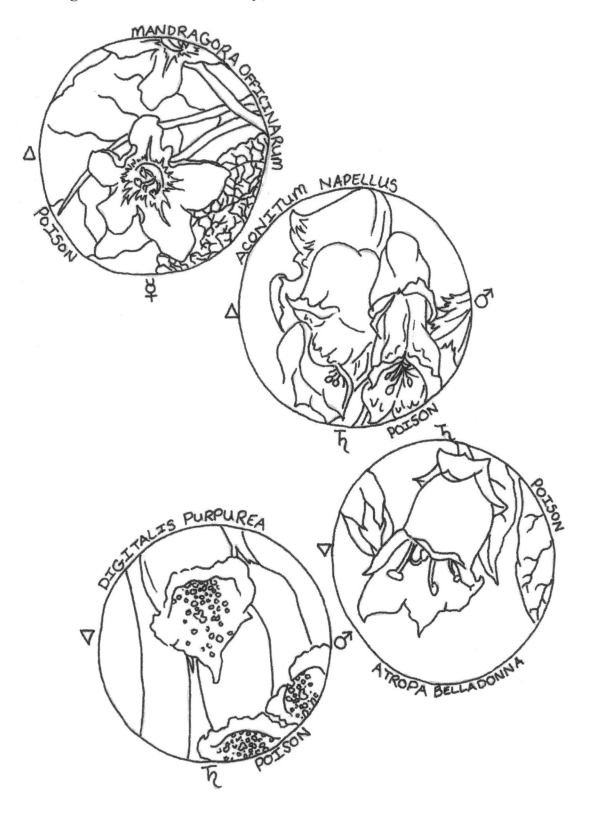

Hekate Einalia rules over the parts of the sea where few things roam. This is also a place where the waves stand like buildings over our tiny vessels, and the crests are whipped like cream. Symbolically this domain also highlights Hekate's dominion over our deepest emotions. The Japanese artist Hokusai inspired the waves that Hekate directs in this illustration.

Hekate was adopted by the Romans, where she was called Hecate Trivia, 'of the Three Roads.' Her mastery of thresholds made her a perfect match with the God Janus, who also ruled thresholds. His two-faced figure also guarded the transition of the years. His gate remains a thing of beauty in Rome.

There are many aspects to the Goddess of Crossroads, Hekate. Her earliest surviving image is of a woman sitting on a throne. She grew to become the Titaness who can cross all boundaries, who has power over many domains, and who continues to enlighten her followers today.

It is not possible to capture the full breadth of Hekate's story and domains in such a short book, but you'll find many resources in the bibliography. My gratitude to each of you who has brought this small offering to Her into your lives. May Her torches guide you well and true!

Primary Sources:

Apollodorus. Library, 1.6.2.

Aristophanes. Frogs and Other Plays (Penguin Classics), David Barret, trans. Penguin, 2007.

Athanassakis, Apostolos N. trans. The Homeric Hymns: Translation, Introduction, and Notes, Johns Hopkins, 2004.

--------. Hesiod: Theogony, Works and Days, Shield, Johns Hopkins, 2004.

---------. The Orphic Hymns, Johns Hopkins, 2013.

Boyle, A.J. Seneca: Medea. Oxford, 2014.

Euripides. Ion, Line 1049.

-----------. Phoenician Women, lines 109-110.

-----------. "Hymn to Hekate," The Trojan Women.

Habicht, Christian. Pausanias' Guide to Ancient Greece (Sather Classical Lectures), University of California, 1999.

Hesiod. Theogony and Works and Days, M.L. West, trans. Oxford, 2009.

Lucian, Pharsalia, 4.839-40.

Ovid. Metamorphoses (Oxford World's Classics), trans. A. D. Melville, Oxford, 2009.

Plato. Six Great Dialogues (Dover Thrift Editions), trans. Benjamin Jowett, Dover, 2007.

Race, William R. Apollonius Rhodius: Argonautica, Loeb Classical Library, 2008.

Strabo, Geography, Vol. VI, Books 13-14 (Loeb Classical Library, No. 223), trans. Horace Leonard Jones, Loeb, 1929.

Theocritus. Idylls (Oxford World's Classics), trans. Anthony Verity, Oxford, 2008.

Virgil. The Aeneid (Penguin Classics), Penguin, 2010. 4.511, 4609-610, 6.247.

West, M. L. The Orphic Poems, Oxford, 1983.

Secondary Sources:

Alcock, S., and R. Osborne, eds. Placing the Gods: Sanctuaries and Sacred Space in Ancient Greece, Oxford, 1994.

Baur, Christopher and Paul Victor. Eileithyia, University of Missouri, 1902.

Berg, William. "Hecate: Greek or 'Anatolian'?" from Numen, Vol. XXI, Fasc. 2, pp. 128-140.

Betz. Hans Dieter. The Greek Magical Papyri in Translation, including the Demotic Spells, Vol. 1, University of Chicago Press, 1992.

Boedeker, Deborah. "Hekate: A Transfunctional Goddess in the Theogony," Transactions of the American Philological Association, 113, 1983, pp. 79-93.

Bremmer, Jan N. Greek Religion, Oxford, 1994.

Burkert, Walter. Greek Religion, trans. John Raffan, Wiley-Blackwell, 1991.

Burns, Dylan. "The Chaldean Oracles of Zoroaster, Hekate's Couch, and Platonic Orientalism in Psellos and Plethon," Aries, vol. 6 no.2, Leiden, 2006. p. 158-179.

Carlsson, Susanne and Lars Karlsson. Labraunda and Karia: Proceedings of the International Symposium Commemorating Sixty Years of Swedish Archaeological Work in Labraunda. Uppsala Universitet, 2008.

Cartledge, Paul et al. Religion in the Ancient Greek City, Cambridge, 1992.

Clauss, James and Sarah Iles Johnston, eds. Medea: Essays on Medea in Myth, Literature, Philosophy and Art, Princeton, 1997.

Clay, Jenny Strauss. "The Hecate of the Theogony" GRBS 25 (2984), pp. 27-38.

--------. Hesiod's Cosmos, Cambridge, 2003.

Daniel, Robert W. "Hekate's Peplos," Zeitschrift fur Papyrologie und Epigraphik, 72, p. 278, 1988.

Dasbacak, C. "Hekate Cult in Anatolia: Rituals and Dedications in Lagina." from Anodos, 6/7 Trnava, 2006/2007.

Drew-Bear, Thomas. "Local Cults in Graeco-Roman Phrygia," Greek, Roman, and Byzantine Studies, Vol. 17, No. 3, 1976. pp. 247-268.

Edwards, Charles M. "The Running Maiden from Eleusis and the Early Classical Image of Hekate," from American Journal of Archaeology, vol. 90, no. 3, (Jul., 1986), pp. 307-318.

Fairbanks, Arthur. "The Chthonic Gods of Greek Religion," The American Journal of Philology, vol. 21, no. 3, 1900, pp. 241-259.

Faraone, Christopher and Dirk Obbink. Magika Hiera: Ancient Greek Magic and Religion, Oxford, 1997.

Graf, Fritz. Magic in the Ancient World (Revealing Antiquity 10), trans. Franklin Philip. Harvard, 1999.

Graf, Fritz and Sarah Iles Johnston. Ritual Texts for the Afterlife: Orpheus and the Bacchic Gold Tablets, Routledge, 2013.

Harrison, Jane E. "Helios-Hades" The Classical Review, vol. 22, issue 1, 1908, pp. 12-16.

Johnston, Sarah Iles. "Animating Statues: A Case Study in Ritual," Arethusa 41, 2008. pp. 445-477.

-----------. "Crossroads" Zeitschrift fur Papyrologie und Epigraphik, 1991, pp. 217-224.

----------. "Demeter, Myths, and the Polyvalence of Festivals," History of Religions, Vol. 52, No. 4, May 2013, editor Wendy Doniger, University of Chicago, 2013.

----------."The Development of Hekate's Archaic and Classical Roles in the Chaldean Oracles," dissertation in pursuit of PhD. at Cornell, 1987.

----------. "Hekate, Leto's Daughter, in OF 317," Tracing Orpheus: Studies of Orphic Fragments, edited by Miguel Herrero de Jauregui, et al., de Gruyter, 2011.

---------. Hekate Soteira: A study of Hekate's Roles in the Chaldean Oracles and Related Literature, American Classical Studies, 1990.

--------. Mantike: Studies in Ancient Divination (Religions in the Graeco-Roman World), Brill, 2005.

--------. Religions of the Ancient World, Harvard, 2004.

--------. Restless Dead: Encounters between the Living and the Dead in Ancient Greece. Univ. of California, 2013.

Kerenyi, Karl. Eleusis: Archetypal Image of Mother and Daughter, trans. Ralph Manheim. Princeton, 1991.

----------. Gods of the Greeks, Thames & Hudson, 1980.

Larson, Jennifer. Ancient Greek Cults: A Guide, Routledge, 2007.

Luck, Georg. Arcana Mundi: Magic and the Occult in the Greek and Roman Worlds: A Collection of Ancient Texts, Johns Hopkins, 2006.

Majercik, Ruth. The Chaldean Oracles: Text, Translation and Commentary, Prometheus Trust, 2013.

Mander, Pietro. "Hekate's Roots in the Sumerian-Babylonian Pantheon according to the Chaldean Oracles," Religion in the History of European Culture: Proceedings of the 9th EASR Annual Conference and IAHR Special Conference 14-17 September 2009, Messina, edited by Giulia Sfameni Gasparro, Augusto Cosentino and Mariangela Monaca. Officina di studi Medievali, 2013, pp. 115-132.

Marquardt, Patricia A. "A Portrait of Hecate," The American Journal of Philology, vol. 102, no. 3 (Autumn, 1981), pp. 243-260.

Mikalson, Jon. D. Ancient Greek Religion, Wiley-Blackwell, 2009.

---------. Athenian Popular Religion, UNC, 1987.

--------. Religion in Hellenistic Athens, Berkeley, 1998.

Nilsson, M.P. Greek Popular Religion, New York, 1940.

Nixon, Shelly M. Hekate: Bringer of Light, California Institute of Integral Studies, 2013

Ogden, Daniel. Magic, Witchcraft and Ghosts in the Greek and Roman Worlds: A Sourcebook, Oxford, 2009.

—————-. Night's Black Agents: Witches, Wizards and the Dead in the Ancient World, Bloomsbury, 2008.

Parker, Robert. Athenian Religion: A History, Oxford, 1996.

---------. Miasma: Pollution and Purification in Early Greek Religion, Oxford, 1990.

Platt, Verity. Facing the Gods: Epiphany and Representation in Graeco-Roman Art, Literature and Religion, Cambridge, 2011.

Pomeroy, S.B. Goddesses, Whores, Wives, and Slaves: Women in Classical Antiquity, New York, 1975.

Rabinowitz, Jacob. Rotting Goddess: The Origins of the Witch in Classical Antiquity. Autonomedia, 1998.

Ronan, Stephen. The Goddess Hekate, Chthonios, 1992.

Sourvinou-Inwood, C. "Reading" Greek Death: To the End of the Classical Period, Oxford 1995.

Tirpan, Ahmet A. "The Temple of Hekate at Lagina," from Dipteros und

Turner, John D. "The Figure of Hecate and Dynamic Emanationism in the Chaldean Oracles, Sethian Gnosticism and Neoplatonism," The Second Century Journal 7;4 . 1991. pp. 221-232.

Von Rudloff, Ilmo Robert. Hekate in Ancient Greek Religion, Horned Owl Pub, 1999.

Williamson, Christina. "Karian, Greek or Roman? The layered identities of Stratonikeia at the sanctuary of Hekate at Lagina," from TMA 50, 2013. p. 1-6.

-------------. "Panamara: The (mis)fortunes of a Karian Sanctuary," from Historische Erfgoed, Groniek, 2009. pp. 211-218.

-------------. "Shining Saviors: The role of the cults of Hekate at Lagina and Zeus at Panamara in building the regional identity of Stratonikeia," Oud Historici Dag, Amsterdam, 2012.

Practitioner's Sources:

Bebout, Tinnekke. Dance of the Mystai, Pagan Writer's Press, 2013.

Bebout, Tinnekke and Hope Ezerins. The Hekate Tarot, self-published, 2015.

Carlson, K. Life's Daughter/Death's Bride: Inner Transformations through the Goddess Demeter/Persephone, Shambhala, 1997.

Conner, Randy P. "Come, Hekate, I Call You to My Sacred Chants," published only on Academia.edu.

Crowfoot, Greg. Crossroads, Aventine Press, 2005.

Crowley, Aleister. Moonchild, Weiser, 1970.

D'Este, Sorita. Artemis: Virgin Goddess of the Sun & Moon: a Comprehensive Guide to the Greek goddess of the Hunt, Her Myths, Powers and Mysteries, Avalonia, 2005.

-------. Hekate Liminal Rites: A study of the rituals, magic and symbols of the torch-bearing Triple Goddess of the Crossroads, Avalonia, 2009.

-------. Hekate: Her Sacred Fires, Avalonia, 2010.

-------. Hekate: Keys to the Crossroads: A collection of personal essays, invocations, rituals, recipes and artworks, Avalonia, 2006.

-------. Horns of Power: Manifestations of the Horned God: An Anthology of Essays exploring the Horned Gods of Myth and Folklore, Ancient History through to ModernTimes, Avalonia, 2011.

Domenic, H. "Who is Hecate?" The Beltane Papers 47, Winter 2009/2010. pp. 9-12, 17-18.

Ford, Michael. Book of the Witch Moon: Chaos, Vampiric & Luciferan Sorcery, Succubus, 2006.

------. Magick of the Ancient Gods: Chthonic Paganism and the Left Hand Path, Succubus, 2009.

George, Demetra. Mysteries of the Dark Moon: The Healing Power of the Dark Goddess, Harper Collins, 1992.

Grimassi, Raven. The Witches' Craft: The Roots of Witchcraft, Llewellyn, 2002.

Jade Sol Luna. Hecate I: Death, Transition and Spiritual Mastery, 2008.

-------. Hecate II: The Awakening of Hydra, 2009.

Keller, M.L. Greek Goddess Traditions and the Eleusinian Mysteries: Spiritual Resources for Today, 2012, In Press.

Marx, E. Junkyard of the Classics, Invisible Books, 2006. (Ellipsis Marx is an alias for Rabinowitz.)

Mishev, Georgi. Thracian Magic: Past and Present, Avalonia, 2012.

Oates, Shani. A Paean for Hekate, Lulu, 2012.

Panopoulos, Christos Pandion, et al. Hellenic Polytheism: Household Worship, Vol. 1, Labrys, 2014.

Payne, Kenn. Askei Kataskei: the Official Covenant of Hekate ezine, vols. 1-6, Covenant of Hekate, Lulu, 2013-2014.

Perdue, Jason. Hecate's Womb (and other Essays), Lulu, 2011.

Rabinowitz, J. The Rotting Goddess: The Origin of the Witch in Classical Antiquity, Autonomedia, 1998.

Reynolds, Tara. Hekate: Goddess Connections Workbook, Kindle, 2013. (17 pages).

Ruickbie, Leo. Witchcraft Out of the Shadows: A Complete History, Hale, 2004.

Sanchez, Tara. The Temple of Hekate: Exploring the Goddess Hekate through Ritual, Meditation and Divination, Avalonia, 2011.

Sannion. Bearing Torches: a Devotional Anthology for Hekate, Bibliotheca Alexandrina, 2009.

Spretnak, Charlene. Lost Goddesses of Early Greece: A Collection of Pre-Hellenic Myths, Beacon, 1992.

Tate, Karen. Sacred Places of Goddess: 108 Destinations. CCC Pub, 2006.

Taylor-Perry, Rosemarie. The God who Comes: Dionysian Mysteries Revisited, Algora, 2003.

Varner, Gary R. Hekate: The Witches' Goddess, Lulu, 2011.

Vermeule, Emily. Aspects of Death in Early Greek Art and Poetry, University of California, 1979.

Winter, Sarah Kate Istra. Kharis: Hellenic Polytheism Explored, 2008.

Printed in Great Britain
by Amazon